FRENCH REGIONAL COOKERY

PROVENCE

Alexandra Doncarli

OCTOPUS BOOKS

Series consultant MARIE-PIERRE MOINE, editor of
TASTE magazine

Project Editor Camilla Simmons
Art Editor Lisa Tai
Editor Anne Johnson
Designer Mike Leaman
Picture Researcher Gale Carlill
Production Controllers Eleanor McCallum,
Mandy Inness

14 Additional recipes supplied by Grund © Grund 1989
Translation of French Lesley Bernstein
Copy editing Jenni Fleetwood
Special Photography Clive Streeter
Food Preparation Eve Dowling, Linda Fraser,
Nichola Palmer, Lyn Rutherford, Jennie Shapter
Styling Marion Price, Sue Russell

The publishers would like to thank the following for their
kind permission to reproduce the following photographs:
Dennis Hughes Gilby: pages 8-9;
Tony Stone Associates: pages 6-7

First published in 1989 by Octopus Books Limited
an imprint of the Octopus Publishing Group
Michelin House
81 Fulham Road
London SW3 6RB

ISBN 0 7064 3100 6

Produced by Mandarin Offset

Printed and bound in Hong Kong

CONTENTS

INTRODUCTION

For the traveller coming from the North, Provence is heralded by the first cicada song near Valence, the first cypresses, the first *'mas'*, or small Provençal house, a scent of thyme, rosemary and lavender and that strong wind, the mistral, which blows down the Rhône valley, clearing clouds and warranting a blue sky. The grass grows thinner and sparser, the earth is dryer, the reflection of the sun more intense, the houses whiter.

However, Provence is not a homogeneous area. It is a land of sharp contrasts, offering at once the landscapes which inspired Cézanne and Van Gogh; and the marshes of the Camargue, the mountains of the Southern Alps, the chalky *calargues* (fjords), and fine sand beaches of the Mediterranean coast.

Long before sun-seekers, painters and novelists looked for inspiration in Provence, others turned their attention towards this part of France.

In the sixth century BC, Greek sailors from Phoenicia established a colony in Marseilles, and were followed by the Romans. Vestiges of their civilization remain. Some are visible; others are still being unearthed on archaeological digs.

The name 'Provence' comes from the Latin word *'provincia'* and the region was a Roman province until 128 BC. Provence is rich in history, as numerous ruins, monuments, names of streets, and customs bear witness. The influence of some events and personages can even be seen in some of the names of local produce such as the wines Châteauneuf du Pape and Muscat des Papes, and confectionery such as *calissons d'Aix du Roy Rene*.

Along the banks of the river Rhône, the soil is fertile and market gardening flourishes producing the many fruits and vegetables for which the region is famous. On the coastline, however, the soil is chalky and poor and is more suitable for vines and olive trees. Here vineyards abound, and if not many of the wines become world renowned vintages they all go well with a plate of local olives and with other foods of the region. In the hinterland, a sparse grass allows sheep and goats to graze. Flowers are grown there also.

On the rocky soil, the *garrigue* (the word for the bushy scrubland of the area) features a profusion of herbs such as sage, lavender, rosemary and thyme. Their leaves produce oils which evaporate under the heat and give Provence its characteristic fragrance. The heat, which pervades Provence, also enhances the taste and flavour of fruit and vegetables and the scent of flowers. All these appear earlier than in other parts of France.

THE PROVENÇAL CUISINE
To understand and appreciate Provençal cuisine, one must first go to the market and see its wealth of

vegetables, fruits and fragrant herbs as well as meats, fish and cheeses.

The Provençal markets are quite different from those found in other regions of France. They are very colourful, pervaded by many sounds and smells, full of strong southern accents and warm humanity. You only have to ask the seller if his fruit is ripe for him to give you a slice of melon, a handful of cherries or half a peach or nectarine to taste.

Perhaps the essence of Provençal cuisine is to be seen and smelt in the bunches of herbs found

One of the many magical scents of Provence, lavender is a symbol of the region. Here it is cultivated at a farm in the hinterland.

throughout the region. These herbs – in particular basil, thyme, rosemary, wild thyme, sage, juniper and fennel – enhance the flavour of Provençal dishes. After herbs, the main ingredients of Provençal dishes are olive oil, tomatoes, garlic, onions, and they are to be found in almost all regional specialities.

Provençal cuisine is not 'haute cuisine' but it belongs to rustic tradition and its preparation as well as its ingredients are conditioned by the seasons and the climate and way of life in Provence.

Soup dishes are hearty, filling and very nourishing. The fish soups with their characteristic strong taste are sometimes served as a whole meal in themselves: *bouillabaisse* and *bourride* are typical examples. Local variations to these dishes, each felt to be authentic, are matters for fierce and passionate feeling.

Mediterranean fish have singing names: *rascasse*, *girelle*, *roucaou*, *merhichon* to name a few, and in their infinite variety lend themselves to many different preparations: grilled on a bed of herbs, baked, *flambés*, boiled, poached, in *terrines*, or *canapés*. They could in fact be a staple diet in coastal regions.

Shellfish are sometimes consumed raw and are not only enjoyed at special occasions and Christmas and New Year celebrations; they are eaten near the fishmonger's stall by *connaisseurs* who do not hesitate in bringing their own white wine with them. Big crates of mussels and sea urchins are everywhere but crabs, crayfish and squid are abundant also at the fishmongers' stalls. *Tautènes farcis*, squid stuffed with spinach or Swiss chard and served with a provençal sauce is a regional dish well worth trying.

Meats are either grilled with herbs or cooked in sauce, marinated like Camargue bull or cooked in their own steam. Of course, some are roasted like leg of lamb, chicken and rabbit. Rabbits fed on thyme have a delicious flesh.

Vegetables ripened in the sun have a particular flavour and are not only used as accompaniments but are served as dishes in their own right: courgettes *au gratin*; stuffed tomatoes, onions, courgettes and aubergines; artichokes *à la barigoule*; grilled peppers. The flowers of some vegetables are also a great delicacy cooked in fritters: most well known are the *beignets de fleurs de courgettes* (courgette-flower fritters).

Rice from the Camargue is usually served with chicken, shellfish and sea-food; it is also the main ingredient of many different salads. The influence of neighbouring Italy is reflected in pizza and pasta dishes as well other specialities.

Because the Provençal vegetation is not favourable to cattle, the cheeses made in the region are mostly goat and ewe's milk cheeses: *brousse, baron*

and *pèbre d'ai*.

Fruit is plentiful and, like the vegetables, fragrant and juicy. On the coast, lemons and oranges scent the air whilst the fertile Vaucluse valleys supply vegetables and fruit not only to the rest of France but to export markets as well. Nowadays, some exotic fruits are grown in Provence: kiwi and passion fruit are very popular.

The fact that fruit is so plentiful has enabled an important preserving industry to flourish: glacé fruit from Apt, jams from Nîmes, confit of almonds from Haute-Provence and all sorts of confectionery specialities such as the previously mentioned *calissons d'Aix*, *nougat* from Montelimar, *berlingots* from Carpentras, *pichoulines* and dried fruit which appear on the Christmas table and make up part of the region's traditional '13 desserts' for Christmas. When fruits are in season, they are also used locally to make tarts and sorbets,

to the great delight of those who have a sweet tooth.

Honey from Haute-Provence is usually scented with the lavender that pervades Provence and is its symbol. Flowers grown in the Grasse area are used in the making of perfumes; some are crystallized and sold at confectioners'. Finally, two liquid products evoke Provence and the Mediterranean basin: olive oil and wine.

Olive oil is used extensively in Provençal dishes. And olives themselves constitute a speciality. Green or black, they come in a great variety and are eaten in as many ways: simply with bread and cheese and a glass of wine; as part of an hors d'oeuvre; as an ingredient in many recipes; or as a garnish to a dish.

Wine is to be found all along the Rhône valley and in Provence. Some wines are famous like the Châteauneuf du Pape, Gigondas, Tavel, Beaumes

A rich variety of vegetables from a market stall in Provence. Tomatoes, peppers, onions and aubergines are at the heart of many Provençal dishes, while rare varieties such as the white aubergines (centre) are also sometimes found.

de Venise. Others are most modest like Vin de Cassis, Bandol, Côteaux d'Aix-en-Provence and the rosé wines traditionally associated with the region. The white wine from Cassis is served with fish and shellfish, rosé from Bandol with hors d'oeuvres, Côtes du Ventoux with red meats and Muscat de Beaumes de Venise with desserts.

And as for an aperitif to conjure up the sun of the South of France, what could be better than the famous *pastis?*

Provençal hors d'oeuvres provide some of the simplest and best pleasures of this cuisine. Many of the dishes are quick and easy to prepare: *Jambon cru aux figues*; tasty anchovy spreads such as *Beurre d'anchois* or *Anchoïde* spread on canapés or toasted on bread to make a *fougasse*; fresh sardines grilled and mashed and used to fill scooped out tomato halves. Also included are more substantial dishes such as *Caillettes* or *Brandade de morue* which take a little more time in the kitchen but are equally typical of the region.

SALADE DE FONDS D'ARTICHAUTS AU FENOUIL
ARTICHOKE HEARTS AND FENNEL SALAD

The best globe artichokes for this recipe are the tiny violets de Provence. The leaves do not have much flesh on them and are not therefore a great loss. Use 6 of these instead of the 3 globe artichokes.

SERVES 4
3 small globe artichokes
juice of 2 lemons
1 medium fennel bulb
1 teaspoon Dijon mustard
50 ml (2 fl oz) olive oil
1 tablespoon chopped chervil to garnish

1 Remove the artichoke leaves and discard. Sprinkle the juice of 1 lemon over the hearts.

2 Cook the artichoke hearts and fennel in boiling water, covered, for 30 minutes. Drain and cool.

3 Slice the artichoke hearts and fennel, and arrange in a salad bowl.

4 Prepare a dressing with the juice of the remaining lemon, the mustard and olive oil, and pour it over the vegetables. Sprinkle with chopped chervil before serving.

SALADE DE FÈVES
BROAD BEAN SALAD

Using only the skinned podded beans in this salad may seem rather laborious, but the colour and flavour make it worthwhile. Use young broad beans when available.

SERVES 6
2.75 kg (6 lb) broad beans in pods
salt and pepper
pinch of sugar
6 whole carrots, peeled (about 500 g/1 lb)
5 spring onions, green tops only
3 tablespoons olive oil
1 tablespoon vinegar

1 Shell the beans and place them in a saucepan of boiling water to cover. Add the salt, pepper and sugar and cook for 30 to 35 minutes adding the carrots 10 minutes after the start of the cooking time.

2 Drain the vegetables. Pop the broad beans out of their skins into a salad bowl. Dice the carrots finely and add to the bowl. Using kitchen scissors, snip the spring onions into the salad.

3 Make a simple vinaigrette by combining the oil and vinegar, with salt and pepper to taste, in a screwtop jar. Shake well, add to the salad and toss lightly. Serve at room temperature.

SALADE DE FÈVES

SALADE NIÇOISE

SALADE NIÇOISE
SALAD NIÇOISE

SERVES 8
2 green peppers
8 medium tomatoes, sliced
225 g (8 oz) French beans, cooked and drained
1 small onion, peeled and finely sliced
1×50 g (2 oz) can anchovy fillets, drained
4 hard-boiled eggs, sliced
225 g (8 oz) tiny black olives
SAUCE VINAIGRETTE:
100 ml (3½ fl oz) olive oil
25 ml (1 fl oz) vinegar
salt and pepper

1 Grill the peppers until the skin blisters, then peel off and discard the skin and slice the peppers.

2 Put all the vegetables, anchovy fillets and slices of egg in a big salad bowl. Add half the olives.

3 Mix the ingredients for the vinaigrette. Pour half on to the salad and toss lightly.

4 Add the rest of the vinaigrette and garnish with the remaining olives.

CÉLERI-RAVE RÉMOULADE
CELERIAC IN MUSTARD SAUCE

SERVES 4
1 celeriac, peeled
juice of 1 lemon
DRESSING:
2 hard-boiled egg yolks
1 raw egg yolk
1 tablespoon Dijon mustard
100 ml (3½ fl oz) olive oil

1 Grate the celeriac into a large bowl. Sprinkle with the lemon juice.

2 To make the rémoulade sauce, crush the hard-boiled egg yolks and mix with the raw egg yolk and Dijon mustard.

Add the oil, drop by drop as when making mayonnaise, and whisk quickly. Alternatively, simply blend all the ingredients in a liquidizer.

3 Pour the dressing over the celeriac and toss well.

POMPE AUX ANCHOIS
ANCHOVY BREAD

SERVES 10
500 g (1 lb) plain flour
1 teaspoon salt
20 g (¾ oz) fresh yeast
2 tablespoons lukewarm water
6 tablespoons olive oil, plus extra for brushing the dough
1×50 g (2 oz) can anchovy fillets, drained

1 Sift the flour and salt into a large mixing bowl. Mash the yeast with the water in a second bowl and set aside until frothy.

2 Make a well in the centre of the flour and add the yeast mixture and the olive oil. Gradually incorporate the flour until a soft, pliable dough is formed. Knead the dough until smooth.

3 Divide the dough in half and roll each piece to a neat oval. (Both ovals should be about the same size.)

4 Place one of the ovals on a baking sheet. Arrange the anchovy fillets on top and cover with the remaining dough oval. Make three cuts in the centre of the dough lid. Cover with a cloth and set aside in a warm place for about 3 hours to rise.

5 Bake the bread in a preheated moderately hot oven, at 200°C (400°F), Gas Mark 6, for 30 minutes, brushing the loaf generously with olive oil halfway through baking. Serve warm as an appetizer with goats' cheese and a well-chilled rosé wine.

SALADE DES PINÈDES
PINE FOREST SALAD

This unusual garden salad can be served either with mayonnaise or with a classic vinaigrette made from olive oil, vinegar and lemon juice.

SERVES 4
100 g (4 oz) curly endive
100 g (4 oz) oak leaf lettuce or rocket
100 g (4 oz) dandelion leaves or lambs lettuce
100 g (4 oz) asparagus tips, steamed
100 g (4 oz) seedless raisins
50 g (2 oz) pine kernels
salt and pepper
salad burnet to garnish
MAYONNAISE:
1 egg yolk, at room temperature
100 ml (3½ fl oz) corn or sunflower oil
1 teaspoon Dijon mustard
salt and pepper

1 Place all the green salad ingredients in a large bowl. Add the raisins and sprinkle with the pine kernels, season with salt and pepper, and toss well.

2 Put all the ingredients for the mayonnaise in a liquidizer and process. Alternatively beat by hand or with an electric whisk adding the oil a little at a time until it is all used up.

3 Finally, garnish the salad with the salad burnet and serve with the mayonnaise.

JAMBON CRU AUX FIGUES
RAW HAM WITH FIGS

SERVES 6
12 ripe green or black figs
6 slices Bayonne or other raw ham,
very thinly sliced

1 Wash all the figs thoroughly. Cut off the stalks and cut crosses in the tops so that they can be opened out.

2 Roll the slices of ham into 6 cone shapes to enclose six of the figs. Arrange these on a platter and decorate with the remaining figs.

PANISSES
CHICKPEA CHIPS

SERVES 6
1 litre (1¾ pints) water
salt and pepper
1½ tablespoons olive oil, plus extra for greasing
300 g (11 oz) chickpea flour
groundnut oil for deep frying

1 Place the water in a saucepan with a little salt and pepper and the olive oil. Bring to the boil, remove from the heat and sprinkle the flour on to the liquid. Mix well with a wooden spatula and return the pan to the heat. Cook, stirring constantly with a wooden spatula, for 5 to 12 minutes or until the mixture is thick and smooth.

2 Pour the mixture into oiled saucers. Dip your fingers into cold water and pack the mixture down tightly. Leave to cool for 3 to 4 hours.

3 Invert the saucers to remove the chickpea mixture. Cut into slices, each about the size of a chip. Heat the groundnut oil in a deep-fat fryer or deep saucepan, add the chickpea chips and fry until golden. Drain on paper towels, transfer to a dish and add salt and pepper to taste. Serve like chips, as an accompaniment to a meat dish.

JAMBON CRU AUX FIGUES

CAILLETTES *(ABOVE)*
OEUFS FARCIS AUX ANCHOIS *(BELOW)*

CAILLETTES
STUFFED PIG'S CAULS

Pig's caul, the lacy membrane around the paunch, is also used to make crépinettes, *small flat sausages made with the best sausagemeat.*

MAKES 1 KG (2 LB)
1 kg (2 lb) spinach or Swiss chard
2-3 teaspoons salt
350 g (12 oz) pig's liver, finely chopped
350 g (12 oz) neck of pork (pork fat), finely chopped
1 medium onion, peeled and finely chopped
4 cloves garlic, crushed
2 tablespoons chopped fresh parsley
120 ml (4 fl oz) white wine
½ teaspoon black pepper
1 pig's caul, soaked in cold water
sage leaves

1 Wash the spinach and discard the stalks. Bring a large saucepan of salted water to the boil, add the spinach leaves and cook for 5 minutes. Drain and immediately plunge the leaves into cold water to arrest the cooking and set the colour. Squeeze the leaves to remove as much water as possible, then chop finely.

2 Combine the pig's liver and neck of pork in a large bowl. Add the spinach, onion, garlic, parsley and white wine. Season with salt and pepper and mix well to make a fairly firm stuffing. Cover and set aside in the refrigerator for at least 8 hours.

3 Drain the pig's caul and spread it out on a work surface. Divide the stuffing into tangerine-sized balls, placing a sage leaf on each. Wrap each ball of stuffing in a piece of the caul and flatten slightly.

4 Arrange the *caillettes* close together on a baking sheet lightly greased with olive oil, with the sage leaves underneath. Bake in a preheated moderately hot oven at 200°C (400°F), Gas Mark 6, for 1½ hours, adding a little beef stock (or vegetable juice or water) from time to time to prevent them burning. Serve hot with a well-seasoned tomato sauce or cold with a green salad.

OEUFS FARCIS AUX ANCHOIS
EGGS STUFFED WITH ANCHOVIES

Preparing the anchovies is a time-consuming operation, so start making this dish at least eight hours before you intend to serve it. If you cannot get salted anchovies, substitute a can of anchovy fillets in olive oil. Drain, reserving the oil, and marinate in a little wine vinegar for about an hour then drain again. Pat dry, return to the oil and proceed with step 2.

SERVES 6
2 oz salted anchovies (see note above)
4 tablespoons wine vinegar (see note)
4 tablespoons olive oil (see note)
6 eggs
salt and pepper
pinch of chopped fresh parsley
TO GARNISH:
lettuce leaves
50 g (2 oz) small black olives

1 Remove the salt from the anchovies: rinse the drained anchovies several times in cold water, drain thoroughly and place in a shallow dish. Add the wine vinegar and marinate the anchovies for 3 to 4 hours. Drain the anchovies again, remove the spines and pat dry between paper towels. Return the anchovies to the clean dish, add the olive oil and soak for 3 to 4 hours.

2 Hard-boil the eggs in salted boiling water for 10 minutes. Plunge them into cold water for 4 to 5 minutes, then shell them.

3 Drain the anchovies, reserving 1 tablespoon of the oil, and place them in a bowl. Cut the hard-boiled eggs in half lengthways. Keeping the whites intact, remove the yolks and add these to the anchovies. Mash well. Add the parsley with pepper to taste and gradually stir in the reserved oil to give a creamy consistency. Stuff the egg whites with this mixture.

4 Arrange the lettuce leaves on a serving dish, place the stuffed eggs on top and garnish with black olives. Serve with radishes, if liked.

ROULEAUX PARADOU
PARADISE ROLLS

This is an easy dish to prepare and makes a simple but smart supper for surprise guests.

SERVES 4
8 thickish slices boiled ham
2 shallots, peeled and finely chopped
25 ml (1 fl oz) vegetable oil
225 g (8 oz) mushrooms, peeled and sliced
50 g (2 oz) butter
200 ml (⅓ pint) fresh double cream
4 tablespoons tomato purée

1 Toss each slice of ham quickly in a non-stick frying pan. Transfer to an ovenproof dish and put to one side.

2 Meanwhile, simmer the finely chopped shallots in the oil for 10 minutes and put to one side. Fry the mushrooms lightly in the butter for 5 minutes. Mix the shallots and mushrooms.

3 Place a tablespoon of the shallot and mushroom mixture on each slice of ham and roll up.

4 Pour the cream into the frying pan and heat very gently. Gradually add the tomato purée and stir well with a wooden spoon.

5 Pour this sauce over the ham rolls and place in a preheated oven, at 180°C (350°F), Gas Mark 4, for 15 minutes.

6 Serve as a starter, or with boiled rice as a main course. A white or rosé wine goes equally well with this dish.

PÂTÉ PROVENÇAL
PROVENÇAL PÂTÉ

For a richer taste, add a tablespoon or so of brandy during the cooking. This pâté will keep for up to aq week in the refrigerator.

FILLS A 500 ML (18 FL OZ) TERRINE
4 tablespoons oil or melted butter
300 g (11 oz) onions, peeled and finely chopped
750 g (1½ lb) chicken livers
1 tablespoon thyme
1½ red peppers
salt and pepper
25 g (1 oz) clarified butter, melted
TO GARNISH:
red pepper
bay leaves
pink peppercorns

1 Put 2 tablespoons of the oil or butter in a frying pan and fry the onions very gently for 20 minutes over a low heat. Drain them and put to one side.

2 Add the remaining oil or butter to the same frying pan. Toss the chicken livers in the thyme and fry quickly for about 5 minutes.

3 Grill the red pepper until the skin blisters, then peel and slice it.

4 When the livers are cool, put them in a liquidizer, food processor or mincing machine with a very fine mesh, along with the fried onions, red pepper, salt and freshly ground pepper.

5 Press the mixture into the terrine and pour over the clarified butter. Decorate the top with thin slices of red pepper cut into diamond shapes, bay leaves and pink peppercorns, then chill in the refrigerator for a few hours. Serve with slices of country bread, gherkins or spring onions, and a Rosé de Provence.

PÂTÉ PROVENÇAL

SARDINES À LA SÉTOISE

SARDINES À LA SÉTOISE
SÉTOISE SARDINES

SERVES 6
6 large tomatoes
salt and pepper
15 fresh medium sardines
100 g (4 oz) butter
3 tablespoons chopped parsley
juice of ½ lemon

1 Halve the tomatoes. Gently scoop out the flesh with a spoon and sprinkle the cases with a little salt. Place in an ovenproof dish in a preheated oven, at 140°C (275°F), Gas Mark 1, for 10 minutes, then drain carefully.

2 Wash and descale the sardines, while patting them dry.

3 Place them under a hot grill for 5 minutes, then turn them and cook for a further 5 minutes. Remove from the heat and mash into a purée, removing the heads and backbone at the same time.

4 Melt the butter in a pan over a low heat. Add the parsley and the sardine purée, season to taste, then add the lemon juice, and heat gently.

5 Stuff the tomatoes with this mixture and serve either hot or cold.

BEURRE D'ANCHOIS
ANCHOVY BUTTER

MAKES 350 G (12 OZ)
175 g (6 oz) anchovy fillets, chopped
175 g (6 oz) unsalted butter
1 small clove garlic, peeled and crushed

1 Place all the ingredients in a mixing bowl and cream together until you have a thick paste.

2 Spread on small toasts; serve with chilled dry white wine as an appetizer.

ANCHOÏADE
A VARIATION ON BEURRE D'ANCHOIS

Short lengths of celery heart, crisped up in iced water, are the traditional accompaniment to this.

SERVES 8
3 × 50 g (2 oz) can anchovy fillets in olive oil
1 clove garlic, peeled and crushed
1 teaspoon chopped basil
1 teaspoon wine vinegar
pepper
additional olive oil, about a tablespoon, to thin

1 Place all the ingredients in a liquidizer and blend thoroughly. Or, if you prefer, you can pound them in a mortar and gradually add the olive oil. Serve as an appetizer with a variety of crudités, or with celery hearts as above, and chilled dry white wine.

2 Alternatively, you can make a *fougasse*: spread the anchoïade on unbaked bread dough, coat it with garlic-flavoured olive oil, and bake in a preheated oven, at 230°C (450°F), Gas Mark 8, for 15 to 20 minutes.

TAPENADE
A VARIATION ON BEURRE D'ANCHOIS

MAKES ABOUT 500 G (1 LB)
2 × 50 g (2 oz) can anchovy fillets in olive oil
100 g (4 oz) capers
225 g (8 oz) black olives, stoned
1 clove garlic, peeled and crushed
3 tablespoons olive oil (including reserved oil)
pepper

1 Drain the anchovy fillets reserving the oil for recipe.

2 Pound the anchovies, capers, olives, and garlic in a mortar and gradually add the olive oil and pepper. Alternatively, use a liquidizer, which will be quicker.

3 Spread the tapenade on small buttered toasts and serve as an *amuse-gueule* or as an accompaniment to hors d'oeuvre.

PIZZA
QUICK PIZZA

SERVES 6 TO 8
400 g (14 oz) self-raising flour
6 tablespoons warm water
½-1 teaspoon salt
6 tablespoons vegetable oil
250 ml (8 fl oz) Coulis de tomates (below)
75 g (3 oz) black olives
1×50 g (2 oz) can anchovy fillets, drained
1 tablespoon oregano
freshly ground pepper

1 Mix the flour with the water, salt and half the oil to prepare a dough.

2 Pour 1 tablespoon of oil into a baking tray, measuring 30 cm (12 inches) square. Roll out the dough and line the tray with it, making sure the dough overlaps the edges by 2 cm (¾ inch). Prick the dough with a fork in several places.

3 Spread the tomato sauce evenly on top. Make a pattern with the olives and anchovies. Sprinkle the oregano on top, along with the remaining oil, and season with freshly ground pepper.

4 Bake in a hot oven, at 230°C (450°F) Gas Mark 8, for 20 to 25 minutes.

COULIS DE TOMATES
THICK TOMATO SAUCE

This sauce can be kept in an airtight container in the refrigerator for 3 to 4 days.

MAKES 300 ML (½ PINT)
6 tablespoons olive oil
3 onions, peeled and finely chopped
1 pinch of sugar
1 kg (2 lb) ripe tomatoes, peeled, seeded and quartered
4 cloves garlic, peeled and finely chopped
salt and freshly ground pepper
2 tablespoons chopped parsley
1 tablespoon chopped basil to garnish (optional)

1 Heat the olive oil in a large frying pan and fry the onions gently for 5 minutes. Add a pinch of sugar.

2 Add the tomatoes, garlic and salt, and boil fast for 10 minutes.

3 Turn down the heat and add the freshly ground pepper. Simmer for another 10 minutes. Add the chopped parsley 3 minutes before the end of the cooking time.

4 Garnish with the chopped basil if it is in season.

PISSALADIÈRE
ONION AND ANCHOVY FLAN

SERVES 4
6 tablespoons olive oil
2 large onions, peeled and sliced
2 cloves garlic, peeled and finely chopped
1 teaspoon sugar
1 bouquet garni
salt and freshly ground pepper
200 g (7 oz) self-raising flour
6 tablespoons warm water
1×50 g (2 oz) can anchovy fillets, drained
75 g (3 oz) black olives

1 Heat 2 tablespoons of olive oil over a gentle heat and fry the onions and garlic gently until soft for 30 minutes. Sprinkle a teaspoon of sugar over them before they turn golden. Add the herbs, salt and pepper.

2 Meanwhile, mix the flour with the warm water, ½ teaspoon of salt and 2 tablespoons of oil to prepare a dough as for a pizza (see opposite). Grease a 23 cm (9 inch) flan dish with 1 tablespoon of oil. Roll out the dough and place it in the dish. Prick with a fork.

3 Spread the fried onions evenly on top. Arrange the anchovies and olives in a lattice pattern. Sprinkle the remaining olive oil over the top and bake in a hot oven, at 220°C (425°C), Gas Mark 7, for 15 minutes.

Pɪssaladière *(above)*
PIZZA *(below)*

B RANDADE DE MORUE *(ABOVE)*
BEIGNETS DE SARDINES *(BELOW)*

BRANDADE DE MORUE
COD MOUSSE

If you have problems obtaining salt cod, 500 g (1 lb) fresh cod fillet, seasoned to taste, provides an acceptable, if less authentic, variation.

SERVES 4
225 g (8 oz) dried salt cod
2 cloves garlic, peeled and crushed
6 tablespoons olive oil
85 ml (3 fl oz) single cream
pepper
juice of 1 lemon
black olives or chopped parsley to garnish
½ *baguette*, sliced and fried

1 Soak the salt cod for 24 to 48 hours, changing the water twice a day. When it is required for cooking, wash the cod well, cut in large pieces and lay in a wide-bottomed pan. Cover with water, bring to the boil slowly, cover the pan and simmer for 8 minutes. Turn off the heat and lift out the fish. Carefully pick out all the bones and skin.

2 Roughly flake the fish and place in a mixing bowl with the garlic. Mix well and gradually add the oil, stirring all the time until you have a rich creamy mixture, or work in the food processor.

3 Place in a saucepan and heat very gently. Add the cream, stirring continuously. Add the pepper and lemon juice. Turn into individual ramekins or a 1.2 litre (2 pint) soufflé dish.

4 Serve cold, garnished with black olives or parsley, and accompanied by a dry white wine. Serve with the fried bread.

BEIGNETS DE SARDINES
SARDINE FRITTERS

A little beer or ale added to the batter mixture in this recipe helps to make the batter light and airy.

SERVES 4
12 small fresh sardines
1 litre (1¾ pints) oil for deep frying
chervil or flat leaf parsley to garnish
BATTER:
175 g (6 oz) plain flour, sifted
salt
1 clove garlic, peeled and crushed
2 eggs
600 ml (1 pint) milk
2 tablespoons beer

1 First prepare the batter. Place the flour, salt and crushed garlic in a large mixing bowl. Break the eggs into a well in the centre and add half the milk. Gradually work in the flour, using a wooden spoon, and beat the mixture until smooth. Gradually add the remaining milk and beat until well mixed and the surface is covered with tiny bubbles. Add the beer and beat well.

2 Descale the sardines. Remove the heads and pull out the backbones. Flatten out the fish and then dip them one by one in the batter.

3 Deep fry in very hot oil until golden brown, then drain the sardines well on kitchen paper.

4 Garnish with chervil or parsley and serve with a twist of lemon.

SOUPS

Robust and nourishing, the soups from this region are often a meal in themselves. They belong to a cuisine whose tradition is comparatively unsophisticated, but rich in natural ingredients and full of flavour. As an antidote, the garlic flavoured broth *Aigo bouludo*, in its simpler versions, offers a cure-all to nervous and over-feasted stomachs.

LA SOUPE AU PISTOU
BEAN SOUP WITH BASIL

In France the haricot beans can be bought fresh, shelled, and simply cooked in the soup with the other ingredients. Dried beans can easily be substituted if fresh are unavailable.

SERVES 8
225 g (8 oz) French beans, sliced
225 g (8 oz) fresh haricot beans, shelled, or dried haricot beans, soaked overnight and precooked for 20 minutes
3 medium courgettes, sliced
4 medium potatoes, peeled and diced
4 medium tomatoes, peeled and seeded
2 litres (3½ pints) hot water
salt and pepper
3 cloves garlic, peeled
15 leaves of basil
1½ tablespoons olive oil
225 g (8 oz) shell pasta
225 g (8 oz) grated cheese to serve

1 Place all the beans, courgettes, potatoes and 3 of the tomatoes in a big cooking pot and cover with the hot water. Season with salt and pepper, bring to the boil and simmer slowly for 45 minutes.

2 Meanwhile, pound the garlic, basil leaves and the remaining tomato together in a bowl. Add the olive oil, mix, and put to one side.

3 Add the pasta to the soup and cook for another 20 minutes.

4 When the soup is cooked, put the reserved mixture of garlic, basil, tomato and oil in the bottom of a soup tureen, add a little of the soup and stir well. Add the rest of the soup and sprinkle with grated cheese just before serving.

AIGO BOULIDO
GARLIC BROTH

Literally translated as boiled garlic water this soothing broth can be enriched with the addition of 2 egg yolks. Beat the yolks in a bowl, gradually mix in a ladleful of the hot broth and add to the soup just before serving.

SERVES 4
1 litre (1¾ pints) water
salt
100 g (4 oz) vermicelli (optional)
6 cloves garlic, peeled and chopped
2 tablespoons olive oil
12–14 slices dry French bread, 1 cm (½ inch) thick

1 Bring the salted water to the boil. Add the vermicelli (if using), garlic and olive oil. Simmer for 15 minutes.

2 Meanwhile, lightly toast the French bread in the oven, put 2 slices in each soup bowl, and pour the soup on top. Replace the toast as necessary.

LA SOUPE AU PISTOU

LA BOUILLABAISSE
MARSEILLES FISH SOUP

This dish is often served as a complete meal in itself. It is, however, impossible to make an authentic bouillabaisse with fish from anywhere other than the Mediterranean although the recipe varies from region to region. Langoustines, for example, are not used in Marseilles but can be found in other Provençal versions of this dish. If you do not have fresh Mediterranean fish available, use the substitutes given below.

SERVES 8
2.5 kg (5½ lb) fish, including at least 6 of the
following:
rascasse (rock fish)
crabe or langoustines
langouste (lobster)
congre (conger eel)
baudroie (or monkfish)
loup (sea bass)
St Pierre (or St Peter's fish)
merlan (whiting)
rouget (red mullet)
moules (mussels)
150 g (5 oz) onions, peeled and sliced
4 cloves garlic, peeled and crushed
2 large tomatoes, peeled, seeded and quartered
1 sprig of thyme
1 sprig of parsley
1 dried fennel stalk
1 bay leaf
1 piece of orange rind
300 ml (½ pint) olive oil
salt and pepper
1 pinch of saffron
ROUILLE:
2 cloves garlic, peeled
2 dried red chillis, peeled and seeded
2 slices of bread, crusts removed, soaked in
milk and squeezed dry
2 tablespoons olive oil
CROÛTONS:
1 small *baguette*, sliced and toasted

1 Ask your fishmonger to clean and descale the fish. Cut them in thick chunks and put them in 2 different dishes: one for firm-fleshed fish, such as rascasse, crabe, langouste, congre and baudroie; and the other for soft-fleshed fish such as loup, St Pierre, merlan and rouget. Scrape the mussels and wash under running cold water.

2 Place the onion, garlic, tomatoes, thyme, parsley, fennel, bay leaf and orange rind in a large pan.

3 Place the firm-fleshed fish on top and pour the olive oil over them. Season with salt and pepper and saffron, stir and leave to marinate for 1 hour.

4 Meanwhile, prepare the *rouille*. Pound the garlic and chillis finely, using a pestle and mortar, or blend in a food processor. Add the slices of bread, then slowly incorporate the olive oil.

5 Cover the marinated fish with boiling water and put the lid on the pan. Cook rapidly over a high heat for just 7 minutes.

6 Add the soft-fleshed fish and quickly put the lid back on the pan. Continue boiling rapidly for a further 5 minutes, adding the mussels at the last moment. It is very important not to exceed the cooking times, as the fish can easily become overcooked. The speed at which the cooking is done enables the oil and fish stock to emulsify perfectly.

7 Arrange the fish in a deep serving dish with the langouste on top.

8 Strain the cooking liquor or *bouillon* into a tureen and add 2 tablespoons to the *rouille* to thin it slightly.

9 Serve with croûtons, a dish of *rouille* and a bowl of grated Gruyère. Each guest, armed with a soup plate, spoon and fork, helps himself first to some fish, a few croûtons and a little of the *rouille*, and then pours some soup or *bouillon* over the top.

LA BOUILLABAISSE

LA BOURRIDE

LA BOURRIDE
FISH SOUP WITH GARLIC SAUCE

Unlike the bouillabaisse, the bourride can easily be prepared outside the Mediterranean, using firm white fish such as whiting, John Dory, grey mullet, halibut, turbot, sea bass and sea bream.

SERVES 6

1.25-1.75 kg (2½-4 lb) fish, such as loup (sea bass), dorade (sea bream), baudroie (monkfish) and merlan (whiting) or mulet (grey mullet)
4 egg yolks, beaten
300 ml (½ pint) Aïoli (see page 35)
24 croûtons
COURT-BOUILLON:
1 onion, peeled and quartered
1 bay leaf
1 piece of lemon peel
1 dried fennel stalk
salt and pepper
6 tablespoons dry white wine
the fish heads

1 First prepare the *court-bouillon* by simmering all the ingredients in 1.2 litres (2 pints) water for 15 minutes. Allow to cool and strain.

2 Clean the fish and cut into good sized slices. Add to the strained *court-bouillon*, bring to the boil and simmer for about 15 minutes until they are all cooked.

3 Stir the beaten egg yolks into half the aïoli and then slowly strain in a ladleful of the *court-bouillon*, whisking constantly until the sauce is thick.

4 Put the croûtons in a serving dish and pour the thick aïoli over them. Place the fish on top, and serve the remaining aïoli separately in a bowl.

SOUPE AUX POIS CASSÉS
SPLIT PEA SOUP

This is a very nourishing soup and could be served as a main course.

SERVES 4

225 g (8 oz) split peas, soaked overnight
1 fresh pig's trotter
1 small slice bacon fat
salt
2 litres (3½ pints) water
2 potatoes, peeled and cubed
2 leeks, sliced
1 small stick celery with leaves, chopped
1 smoked sausage, sliced
6 peppercorns, crushed
1 tablespoon chopped sarriette (savory)

1 Place the peas, pig's trotter, bacon fat and a pinch of salt in a large pan, then pour the water on top and bring to the boil.

2 Half-cover the pan and simmer for 2 to 3 hours, skimming off any excess fat at frequent intervals.

3 Add the potato, leek and celery, and simmer for a further 30 minutes.

4 Lift out the pig's trotter and bacon fat. Remove the bone from the pig's trotter, and dice the meat and the bacon fat. Add these to the soup. Also add the smoked sausage, crushed peppercorns and sarriette.

5 Bring back to the boil quickly and serve in a hot tureen.

FISH AND SHELLFISH

Seafood is plentiful in the coastal regions of Provence: sea bream; cod; red mullet; tuna fish; sea bass; a wide variety of shellfish; and squid. Cod with aïoli, red mullet in a sea urchin sauce, and sea bass or red mullet flamed in pastis are particularly celebrated local combinations, but there are many others to enjoy. And as well as recipes for fresh fish, one of the regional specialities for salt cod, *Morue provençale* is also included here.

DORADE AU FOUR
BAKED SEA BREAM

SERVES 4 TO 6
1 sea bream, weighing about 1-1.25 kg
(2-2½ lb)
1 small onion, peeled and sliced
25 g (1 oz) butter
3 small tomatoes, halved
2 tablespoons fish stock, to taste
100 ml (3½ fl oz) cold water
juice of 1 lemon
1 tablespoon fresh white breadcrumbs
1 tablespoon chopped tarragon leaves
3 tablespoons olive oil
1 lemon, sliced, to garnish

1 Ask your fishmonger to clean and descale the fish, without removing the head. Place in an ovenproof dish.

2 Fry the onion gently in the butter over a low heat for about 15 minutes, or until golden brown.

3 Arrange the halved tomatoes and the fried onion around the fish. Pour the fish stock, water and lemon juice over the fish. Finally, sprinkle with the breadcrumbs, chopped tarragon and olive oil.

4 Bake in a preheated moderate oven, at 180°C (350°F), Gas Mark 4, for 40 to 45 minutes, basting occasionally.

5 Garnish with lemon slices just before serving.

DORADE FARCIE
STUFFED SEA BREAM

SERVES 4 TO 6
1 sea bream, weighing about 1-1.25 kg
(2-2½ lb)
2 slices white bread, soaked in milk
100 g (4 oz) slice whiting, soaked in milk, then flaked
350 g (12 oz) button mushrooms, sliced
1 medium onion, peeled and chopped
1 tablespoon chopped parsley
1 egg, beaten
200 ml (⅓ pint) dry white wine
salt and pepper

1 Ask your fishmonger to descale and clean the bream, without removing the head.

2 Squeeze the bread dry and add the flaked whiting, the mushrooms, onion, parsley and beaten egg.

3 Place this stuffing inside the sea bream and sew the fish up securely with cotton.

4 Place the fish in an ovenproof dish, and pour over the wine and a little water. Season with salt and pepper.

5 Bake in a preheated moderate oven, at 180°C (350°F), Gas Mark 4, for 45 to 50 minutes, basting from time to time.

DORADE AU FOUR

Morue Provençale *(ABOVE)*
THON AUX POIVRONS *(BELOW)*

GRAND AÏOLI
COD WITH GARLIC SAUCE

SERVES 4
1 kg (2 lb) cod steaks
225 g (8 oz) carrots, peeled and halved
500 g (1 lb) medium potatoes, peeled and
halved
2 litres (3½ pints) cold water
AÏOLI:
3 cloves garlic, peeled and chopped
1 egg yolk
1 teaspoon Dijon mustard
salt and pepper
300 ml (½ pint) olive oil

1 Place the fish and vegetables in a large pot and cover with the cold water. Bring to the boil, cover and simmer for 20 to 30 minutes.

2 Meanwhile, prepare the sauce. Pound the garlic in a bowl, add the egg yolk, mustard, salt and pepper. Stir and gradually incorporate the oil, stirring continually with a wooden spoon as when making mayonnaise.

3 Drain the fish and vegetables and arrange on a serving dish, accompanied by the aïoli in a sauceboat.

MORUE PROVENÇALE
SALT COD PROVENÇALE

SERVES 4
1 kg (2 lb) salt cod
2 medium onions, peeled and sliced
500 g (1 lb) potatoes, peeled and thickly sliced
4 large tomatoes, peeled, seeded and quartered
3 cloves garlic, peeled and crushed
50 g (2 oz) capers
100 g (4 oz) black olives, stoned
600 ml (1 pint) dry white wine
1 tablespoon chopped basil
1 bay leaf
2 tablespoons olive oil
pepper
1 tablespoon chopped parsley to garnish

1 Soak the salt cod overnight to remove the salt. Rinse well and drain.

2 Cut the cod in large chunks and place in a big earthenware casserole. Cover this with a layer of onions, then one of potatoes and one of tomatoes, and finally the garlic. Add the capers, olives and wine. Sprinkle with the basil, add the bay leaf, season with olive oil and pepper, and cover.

3 Bake in a preheated moderate oven, at 200°C (400°F), Gas Mark 6, for about 1¼ to 1½ hours or until tender. Sprinkle with chopped parsley just before serving.

THON AUX POIVRONS
TUNA FISH WITH GREEN PEPPERS

SERVES 4 TO 6
1 kg (2 lb) fresh tuna steaks, cut 2 cm (¾ inch)
thick and dusted with seasoned plain flour
6 tablespoons olive oil
2 green peppers
2 medium onions, peeled and sliced
2 large tomatoes, quartered
1 clove garlic, peeled and crushed
1 bouquet garni
200 ml (⅓ pint) dry white wine

1 Gently fry the floured tuna steaks in half the olive oil. Place in an ovenproof dish.

2 Meanwhile, place the green peppers under the grill until the skin blisters, then remove it and slice the peppers.

3 Fry the onions gently in the remaining olive oil until golden brown and very tender. Add the green pepper, tomatoes, garlic and bouquet garni. Season to taste. Simmer for 20 minutes. Add the wine. Return to the boil.

4 Cover the tuna steaks with the sauce. Bake in a preheated hot oven, at 200°C (400°F), Gas Mark 6, for 20 minutes, then cover and cook for a further 30 minutes, at 160°C (325°F), Gas Mark 3.

ROUGETS À L'OURSINADE
RED MULLET IN SEA URCHIN SAUCE

In France the rougets are usually cooked without gutting for this dish, as the liver is considered a great delicacy. If you prefer, you can cook them gutted. They will still taste delicious.

SERVES 6
6 red mullet
3 tablespoons olive oil
3 dried fennel stalks
SAUCE:
36 sea urchins
juice of 1 lemon
pepper

1 Ask your fishmonger to descale the fish and to clean and gut them if you wish.

2 Pat the fish dry with kitchen paper and place in a deep dish. Sprinkle the olive oil on top and allow to stand in a cool place for 1 hour. Meanwhile, preheat the grill.

3 Grill the fish on a bed of fennel stalks for 15 minutes, turning once.

4 To make the sauce, open the sea urchins and remove the corals. Blend with the lemon juice and pepper in a liquidizer.

5 Warm the sauce over a gentle heat taking care that it does not boil.

6 When the fish are cooked, arrange them on a serving dish and pour the sea urchin sauce over them.

ROUGETS AU RICARD
RED MULLET WITH RICARD

The delicate flavour of Ricard works better with this dish than that of Pernod, although Pernod can be substituted. Ricard is, in any case, reputed to be the 'genuine pastis of Marseilles'.

SERVES 4
8 small red mullet, scaled and cleaned
3 tablespoons Ricard
1 tablespoon herbes de Provence
100 g (4 oz) butter, melted
200 ml (⅓ pint) double cream

1 Sprinkle the mullet with 2 tablespoons of Ricard (or with Pernod, if using) and the herbes de Provence. Allow to macerate for 10 minutes.

2 Preheat the grill to medium. Grill the fish for 6 minutes on each side.

3 Meanwhile, prepare the sauce. Warm 1 tablespoon of Ricard in a ladle, pour it over the melted butter, and flame. Reduce the sauce a little, then add the cream and reduce again.

4 When the fish is cooked, arrange on a serving dish and pour the sauce over the top. Serve with plain boiled potatoes and with steamed mangetout, and a dry white wine to drink.

ROUGETS AU RICARD

LOUP AU FENOUIL
SEA BASS WITH FENNEL

Sea bass, grilled on fennel and flamed with a little brandy, turns a simple dish into something uniquely special. Pastis could be used instead of Cognac, to impart a different flavour.

SERVES 4

1 sea bass, weighing about 750 g-1 kg (1½-2 lb)
2 tablespoons olive oil
4 dried fennel stalks
2 tablespoons Cognac

1 Ask your fishmonger to descale and clean the fish.

2 Make 2 slanting incisions with a sharp knife across both sides and sprinkle with the olive oil.

3 Place the fennel stalks under a hot grill and put the sea bass on top of them. Grill for about 20 minutes, turning it over twice during the cooking.

4 When the sea bass is cooked, transfer it and the fennel to a flameproof serving dish.

5 Warm the Cognac in a ladle, flame and pour over the fish. The fennel should catch fire and impart a delicate flavour to the fish.

CALAMARS À LA PROVENÇALE
SQUID, PROVENÇAL-STYLE

SERVES 8

2.5 kg (5½ lb) squid
2 tablespoons groundnut oil
3 onions, peeled and chopped
4 cloves garlic, peeled and crushed
300 g (11 oz) tomato purée
2 tablespoons olive oil, plus extra to finish dish
3 tablespoons brandy
250-300 ml (8-10 fl oz) white wine
salt and pepper
2 tablespoons chopped fresh parsley
pinch of saffron

1 Wash the squid, cut off the tentacles, throw away the beak and the quill. Chop the sacs into thin, flat pieces and the tentacles into 2 cm (¾ inch) lengths.

2 Heat the squid and tentacles in a dry frying pan over high heat for about 5 minutes. When they curl up and turn pink, drain, reserving the juices. Set the squid aside.

3 Heat the groundnut oil in a large saucepan, add the onion and garlic and sauté for 4 to 5 minutes until golden. Stir in the tomato purée and reserved squid liquid. Bring the liquid to the boil, lower the heat and simmer while frying and flaming the squid.

4 Heat the olive oil in a frying pan, add the reserved squid and cook for 2 to 3 minutes, then add the brandy and flame.

5 When the flames die down, transfer the squid to the sauce, sprinkle with white wine, and add salt, pepper and parsley. Simmer for 45 minutes. If necessary, add more liquid in the form of white wine or vegetable stock.

6 Just before serving, add the saffron and a dash of oil. Serve with a ring of rice. A Provençal rosé wine is an excellent accompaniment.

CALAMARS À LA PROVENÇALE

TAUTÈNES FARCIS
STUFFED SQUID

SERVES 6
200 g (7 oz) fresh white breadcrumbs
250 ml (8 fl oz) water
6-12 small squid
500 g (1 lb) Swiss chard, green parts only, or
spinach
1 tablespoon olive oil
1 small onion or shallot, peeled and chopped
2 cloves garlic, crushed
1 tablespoon chopped fresh parsley
2 egg yolks
salt and pepper
TOMATO SAUCE:
1 tablespoon olive oil
1 onion, peeled and chopped
2 cloves garlic, crushed
500 g (1 lb) tomatoes, skinned and chopped
1 bouquet garni
salt and pepper

1 Place the breadcrumbs in a shallow bowl. Add the water and soak for 15 minutes. Drain, squeezing the bread to extract as much liquid as possible. Set aside.

2 Wash the squid, cut off the tentacles and throw away the quill and beak. Reserve the bodies of the squid for stuffing. Chop the tentacles and set aside in a large bowl.

3 Cook the Swiss chard or spinach in a large saucepan of boiling water for 5 minutes. Drain, refresh in cold water, then drain again, squeezing the leaves to extract as much liquid as possible. Chop the leaves finely and add to the chopped squid.

4 Heat the oil in a frying pan, add the onion or shallot and fry for 5 to 6 minutes until brown. Stir into the squid and chard mixture together with the garlic, reserved breadcrumbs, parsley and egg yolks. Season with salt and pepper.

5 Stuff each squid about two-thirds full, sewing the openings closed with needle and thread. Place the stuffed squid, close together, on a shallow oiled baking dish.

6 To make the sauce, heat the oil in a large frying pan, add the onion and garlic and sauté for 4 to 5 minutes until golden. Stir in the tomatoes, bouquet garni, salt and pepper. Leave to reduce over a low heat for 10 minutes. Do not cover the pan. Remove the bouquet garni and purée the sauce in a blender.

7 Pour the tomato sauce over the squid and cook in a preheated moderate oven, at 180°C (350°F), Gas Mark 4, for 30 minutes. Remove the bouquet garni and serve.

MOULES FARCIES
STUFFED MUSSELS

SERVES 4
24 large or 28 smaller mussels
200 ml (⅓ pint) water
1 glass dry white wine
1 tablespoon chopped parsley
1 bouquet garni
pepper
100 g (4 oz) dry breadcrumbs
1 tomato, finely chopped
2 shallots, peeled and finely chopped
3 cloves garlic, peeled and finely chopped
1 tablespoon chopped chives
50 g (2 oz) butter

1 Wash the mussels well in running cold water and scrape the shells.

2 Bring the water to the boil in a large pan with the wine, parsley, bouquet garni and pepper. Add the mussels, cover and cook for about 4 minutes until they open. Then remove the cooked mussels from their shells, and discard any that haven't opened.

3 Chop the mussels and mix them with 75 g (3 oz) of the breadcrumbs, the tomato, shallots, garlic, chives and butter.

4 Stuff the empty shells with this mixture and place in an ovenproof dish. Sprinkle the remaining breadcrumbs on top and brown for 10 minutes in a preheated oven, at 200°C (400°F), Gas Mark 6. Serve immediately.

MOULES FARCIES

PILAF DES PÊCHEURS

PILAF DES PÊCHEURS
FISHERMEN'S PILAF

SERVES 6

3 live crabs or 2 live crabs and 6 live baby crabs
225 g (8 oz) small squid, cleaned and sliced
4 tablespoons olive oil
salt and pepper
3 large tomatoes, peeled, seeded and quartered
2 onions, peeled and sliced
50 g (2 oz) butter
225 g (8 oz) rice
1 pinch saffron
2 litres (3½ pints) fresh mussels
COURT-BOUILLON:
2 litres (3½ pints) water
1 bouquet garni
salt and pepper

1 Prepare a *court-bouillon* with the water, bouquet garni, salt and pepper. Boil for 10 minutes before adding all the crabs, then simmer for a further 10 minutes.

2 Drain the crabs, reserving the *court-bouillon*, and allow to cool before opening the shells and removing the crab meat.

3 Fry the sliced squid gently in 1 tablespoon of olive oil for 5 minutes. Season with salt and pepper.

4 Fry the quartered tomatoes gently in 1 tablespoon of oil until soft.

5 Gently fry the onions in the butter and the remaining oil until golden brown and very soft.

6 Add the rice to the onions, stirring well with a wooden spoon. Gradually pour in the *court-bouillon* and cook until the rice has absorbed it.

7 When the rice is nearly cooked, add the fried squid and tomatoes, and the saffron. Season with salt and pepper.

8 Meanwhile, immerse the mussels in a pan of boiling water. Cover and boil for about 4 minutes until they open (discard any that don't). Remove the flesh from the shells and set aside. Strain the cooking juice and add a ladleful to the rice.

9 Finally, add the mussels and crab meat to the rice and serve very hot.

QUEUES DE LANGOUSTE À LA PROVENÇALE
CRAWFISH TAILS WITH PARSLEY AND GARLIC

SERVES 4

4 crawfish or lobster tails (about 150 g/5 oz each)
court-bouillon to cover (see opposite)
salt and pepper
SAUCE:
4 cloves garlic, peeled and crushed
225 g (8 oz) butter
1 tablespoon chopped parsley

1 Poach the crawfish tails for 7 minutes in the *court-bouillon*.

2 Make the garlic butter sauce by pounding all the ingredients together.

3 Shell the crawfish tails and place in an ovenproof dish. Season with salt and pepper and cover with the garlic butter.

4 Place in a preheated moderately hot oven, at 220°C (425°F), Gas Mark 7, for 10 minutes. Serve on a bed of plain boiled rice.

Provençal meat and poultry dishes have their own unique flavour, imparted from the many herbs growing wild throughout the region. *Roti de porc à la sauge* and *Canard du pays niçois* are some impressive speciality dishes. Also traditional are casseroles of lamb or beef, cooked slowly in a *cocotte* or *fait tout* until the meat is meltingly tender.

POULET AUX HERBES ET AUX OLIVES
CHICKEN WITH HERBS AND OLIVES

SERVES 4
175 g (6 oz) black olives, stoned
1 tablespoon chopped parsley
1 tablespoon chopped chervil
1 tablespoon chopped tarragon
1 tablespoon chopped watercress
3 cloves garlic, peeled and chopped
150 g (5 oz) butter, melted
salt and pepper
1 chicken, about 1.25-1.5 kg (2½-3 lb) weight
3 tablespoons olive oil
bouquet garni of fresh seasonal herbs

1 Chop half the black olives and mix with all the fresh herbs, watercress, garlic and butter. Season with salt and pepper.

2 Rub the mixture over the chicken pieces.

3 Place the chicken in an ovenproof dish, prick the skin all over with a sharp knife, and sprinkle with the olive oil.

4 Roast in a preheated oven, at 200°C (400°F), Gas Mark 6, for 35 to 45 minutes.

5 Garnish with the remaining olives and remove the bouquet garni just before serving. Serve with any green vegetable.

POULET AU CITRON
CHICKEN WITH LEMON

SERVES 4
1 chicken, about 1.5-1.75 kg (3-4 lb) weight
juice of 1 lemon
3 tablespoons olive oil
25 g (1 oz) butter, melted
salt and pepper
1 pinch of herbes de Provence
1 lemon, peeled and sliced
lemon slices to garnish

1 Brush the chicken all over with the lemon juice.

2 Mix 2 tablespoons of olive oil with the butter, salt, pepper and herbes de Provence, and coat the chicken with this sauce.

3 Place the peeled lemon slices inside the chicken. Roast in a preheated moderate oven, at 180°C (350°F), Gas Mark 4, for 1 to 1½ hours.

4 Sprinkle with the remaining olive oil just before serving, garnish with the lemon slices and serve with plain boiled rice or with fresh peas and baby carrots.

POULET AUX HERBES ET AUX OLIVES

DAUBE DE LAPIN DES BASSES-ALPES
BASSES-ALPES RABBIT STEW

The essence of a 'daube' is long slow cooking, so use a good quality, heavy cooking pot with a close fitting lid.

SERVES 6

150 g (5 oz) dried boletus mushrooms
1×2 kg (4½ lb) rabbit, cut into serving portions
salt and pepper
2 tablespoons groundnut oil
2 large onions, peeled and chopped
4 cloves garlic, crushed
3 medium carrots, chopped
½ stick celery, chopped
500 ml (18 fl oz) red wine

1 Soak the dried mushrooms in lukewarm water to cover for 30 minutes.

2 Meanwhile, season the rabbit portions with salt and pepper. Heat the oil in a large saucepan, add the rabbit portions and brown quickly on all sides. With a slotted spoon, remove the rabbit and set the portions aside.

3 Add the onions, garlic, carrots and celery to the oil remaining in the pan. Cook for 2 to 3 minutes, then stir in the wine. Return the portions of rabbit to the pan, spooning the sauce over them. Cover the pan and simmer for 45 minutes.

4 Drain the mushrooms, slice them finely and add them to the pan with salt and pepper to taste. Simmer the stew for 45 minutes more. Serve with fresh pasta, if liked.

LAPIN À LA DIABLE
DEVILLED RABBIT

SERVES 4 OR 5

1 rabbit, weighing about 1.5 kg (3 lb)
225 g (8 oz) bacon, rinded and cut into strips
1×50 g (2 oz) can anchovy fillets, drained
freshly ground pepper
1 tablespoon chopped parsley
1 bunch of chives, chopped
2 shallots, peeled and chopped
50 g (2 oz) butter, softened
1 tablespoon olive oil
1 cup chicken stock
juice of 1 lemon
MARINADE:
6 tablespoons olive oil
2 tablespoons wine vinegar
4 bay leaves
2 sprigs of parsley
2 onions, peeled and chopped
salt

1 Cut the rabbit into joints. Combine all the marinade ingredients and marinate the rabbit in the refrigerator for 2 hours, turning occasionally.

2 Lift the rabbit pieces out of the marinade with a slotted spoon, cut slits in the meat with a sharp knife and insert the bacon strips and anchovy fillets in the slits. Season with freshly ground pepper.

3 Strain the marinade through a fine sieve. Put the rabbit pieces in a pan, add the strained marinade, cover and simmer gently for 1¼ hours. Remove the meat and keep warm.

4 Add the chopped parsley, chives, shallots, softened butter, olive oil and chicken stock to the cooking liquor. Simmer gently, stirring continuously with a wooden spoon, until the sauce has thickened. Then add the lemon juice, boil fast for a few minutes, and pour the sauce over the meat. Serve with steamed or boiled potatoes garnished with parsley, or with sauté potatoes, and a strong red wine from Provence.

LAPIN À LA DIABLE

DAUBE DES GARDIANS *(ABOVE)*
ALOUETTES SANS TÊTE *(BELOW)*

POT-AU-FEU PROVENÇAL
PROVENÇAL BEEF CASSEROLE

SERVES 4
1.5 litres (2½ pints) water
salt
500 g (1 lb) shin of beef
1 marrow bone
2 large onions, peeled and halved
10 small carrots, peeled
5 medium potatoes, peeled
5 small parsnips, peeled
1 stick celery

1 Bring the water to the boil, add the salt, beef and marrow bone, then reduce the heat and simmer for 2 hours.

2 Skim off excess fat, add all the vegetables and simmer for another 30 minutes.

3 The consommé is served first with slices of French bread, and is then followed by the meat and vegetables. Traditionally, the meat is eaten with either coarse sea salt or Dijon mustard.

DAUBE DES GARDIANS
BEEF CASSEROLE FROM THE CAMARGUE

SERVES 6 TO 8
2 kg (4½ lb) shin of beef or blade
salt and freshly ground pepper
1 bottle Côtes du Rhône
1 piece of bacon rind
500 g (1 lb) onions, peeled and sliced
500 g (1 lb) tomatoes, peeled, seeded and quartered
3 cloves garlic, peeled and crushed
1 bouquet garni

1 Dice the meat evenly into bite-sized pieces and place in an earthenware dish with the salt, pepper and red wine. Leave to marinate in the refrigerator overnight.

2 The following day, lift out the meat with a slotted spoon, transfer it to a casserole with the bacon rind, and alternate layers of meat with layers of sliced onion. Place the tomatoes on top, add the garlic and bouquet garni, and strain the marinade into the pot.

3 Bring to the boil, reduce the heat and simmer gently for 4 hours. Remove the bacon rind. Serve with boiled potatoes and another bottle of Côtes du Rhône!

ALOUETTES SANS TÊTE
BEEF OLIVES

SERVES 4
225 g (8 oz) streaky bacon, rinded and finely chopped
4 onions, peeled and finely chopped
4 cloves garlic, peeled and finely chopped
1 tablespoon chopped parsley
1 tablespoon chopped basil
8 very thin slices topside of beef
3 tablespoons olive oil
1 litre (1¾ pints) red wine
100 g (4 oz) tomato purée

1 Combine the chopped bacon, onions, garlic, parsley and basil, and stir well.

2 Place 2 tablespoons of this stuffing in the centre of each slice of beef, roll up into a parcel shape and tie with fine string.

3 Heat the olive oil in a casserole and brown the beef olives lightly all over for 5 minutes.

4 Add the red wine and tomato purée. Simmer gently for 1 hour. Serve with tagliatelle, sprinkled with grated cheese, and a bottle of good red wine from Provence.

BIFTECKS HACHÉS AUX HERBES
HAMBURGERS WITH HERBS

SERVES 4
500 g (1 lb) skirt or sirloin steak, minced
1 tablespoon chopped parsley
1 pinch of thyme
1 shallot, peeled and finely chopped
1 clove garlic, peeled and finely chopped
salt and pepper
plain flour or beaten egg to bind

1 Combine the minced beef with the herbs, shallot and garlic, and season with salt and pepper. Mix in a little plain flour or beaten egg to bind.

2 Divide the mixture into 4 equal parts and shape into hamburgers.

3 Cook under a moderate grill for 8 to 10 minutes on each side. Serve with Pâtes à la tomate et aux champignons (see page 66).

ROMSTECK AUX ANCHOIS
RUMPSTEAK WITH ANCHOVIES

SERVES 4
4 slices rumpsteak or sirloin, each weighing
175-225 g (6-8 oz)
1 tablespoon olive oil
salt and pepper
1×50 g (2 oz) can anchovy fillets, drained
4 large green olives

1 Sprinkle the steaks with olive oil and grill under a hot grill for 2 minutes on each side.

2 Season with a little salt and pepper, and garnish with the anchovy fillets, arranged in a criss-cross pattern, and one olive on each steak. Serve with *pommes de pailles* (matchstick potatoes).

LANGUE DE BOEUF EN SAUCE PIQUANTE
OX TONGUE IN HOT SAUCE

SERVES 6
1 ox tongue
1 leek, sliced
2 carrots, peeled and sliced
1 stick celery, sliced
1 large onion, peeled and stuck with 2 cloves
1 sprig of thyme
1 bay leaf
salt and pepper
2 tablespoons chopped parsley to garnish
SAUCE:
1 medium onion, peeled and finely chopped
3 tablespoons olive oil
1 tablespoon plain flour
300 ml (½ pint) dry white wine
1½ tablespoons wine vinegar
6 small gherkins, finely chopped
1 tablespoon capers
6 tablespoons tomato purée

1 Soak the tongue in cold water for 3 hours, then drain.

2 Place it in a large cooking pot containing 2 litres (3½ pints) of water, and bring to the boil. Continue to boil for 20 minutes.

3 Rinse under cold running water, drain and peel.

4 Prepare a vegetable stock with all the vegetables, thyme, bay leaf, salt and pepper, and 3 litres (5½ pints) of water. Add the tongue, bring back to the boil and simmer gently for 1¾ hours.

5 Meanwhile, prepare the sauce. Lightly fry the chopped onion in olive oil until soft, sprinkle with flour and stir. Add the wine, vinegar, chopped gherkins, capers and tomato purée, and simmer for 5 minutes.

6 When the tongue is cooked, place it on a serving dish and cut into slices. Pour a little sauce on top and garnish with parsley. Serve the remaining sauce in a sauceboat.

LANGUE DE BOEUF EN SAUCE PIQUANTE

G IGOT FARCI À L'AIL *(ABOVE)*
BROCHETTES DE MOUTON *(BELOW, RECIPE ON PAGE 56)*

ESTOUFFADE D'AGNEAU
LAMB CASSEROLE

SERVES 6
1.25 kg (2½ lb) shoulder of lamb (boned and
trimmed weight), diced
1 large onion, peeled and finely chopped
2 cloves garlic, peeled and crushed
2 large tomatoes, peeled, seeded and quartered
1 bouquet garni
zest of 1 orange, cut into thin strips
salt and freshly ground pepper
1 bottle red wine
2 tablespoons olive oil
225 g (8 oz) streaky bacon, rinded and diced
300 ml (½ pint) chicken stock
225 g (8 oz) plain flour

1 Remove any excess fat from the diced meat. Place the meat in a large casserole with the chopped onion, crushed garlic, tomatoes, bouquet garni, orange zest and 1 teaspoon of pepper. Pour the wine on top, add the oil and stir. Allow to marinate in the refrigerator for 4 hours.

2 Meanwhile, blanch the bacon in boiling water for 2 minutes and drain. Next, add the bacon and chicken stock to the marinade so that the meat is well covered with the liquid. Add a pinch of salt.

3 Mix the flour with a little water and roll the resultant paste into a thin strip. Put the lid on the casserole and press the strip of flour paste between the dish and lid to form a seal.

4 Cook in a preheated oven, at 200°C (400°F), Gas Mark 6, for 1 hour, then reduce to 180°C, (350°F) Gas 4, for a further 2 hours. Discard the strip of baked flour and remove the bouquet garni. Transfer the casserole to a serving dish and serve with rice, cooked with red and green peppers, and a good bottle of strong red wine.

GIGOT FARCI À L'AIL
LEG OF LAMB STUFFED WITH GARLIC

SERVES 6
1.75 kg (4 lb) leg of lamb
100 g (4 oz) butter
3 cloves garlic, peeled and finely chopped
2 tablespoons chopped parsley
salt and pepper

1 Ask your butcher to bone the meat and remove any fat.

2 Cream the butter with the garlic and parsley, and season with salt and pepper. Roll this mixture in aluminium foil and place in the refrigerator for 1 hour or until firm. Then remove the foil and stuff the meat with the butter, garlic and parsley roll. Sew up both ends of the meat with thread and tie with fine string to keep its shape.

3 Place the joint in a roasting tin and cook in a preheated oven, at 230°C (450°F), Gas Mark 8. When the meat is golden brown, after about 15 minutes, reduce the temperature to 190°C (375°F), Gas Mark 5 and cook for a further 1–1¼ hours.

4 Turn off the oven, open the oven door and leave it ajar to allow the meat to rest for a few minutes before carving. Serve with gravy made from the roasting juices, Ratatouille (see page 62) or green flageolet beans and a Rosé de Provence.

BROCHETTES DE MOUTON
LAMB KEBABS

SERVES 4
575 g (1¼ lb) fillet or top leg of lamb
1 onion, peeled and quartered
1 green pepper, seeded and diced
2 large tomatoes, quartered
12 mini chipolata sausages
salt and pepper
olive oil in which sprigs of thyme have
marinated

1 Dice the meat into about 16 pieces. Thread the lamb on to skewers, alternating with onion, green pepper, tomato and chipolatas. Season with salt and pepper and sprinkle with the olive oil.

2 Cook the kebabs under a hot grill for 10 to 12 minutes, turning them frequently, and serve on a bed of rice with a Coulis de tomates (see page 22).

CARBONNADO
CARBONNADE OF LAMB

SERVES 6
6 thick lamb leg steaks, 100-150 g (4-5 oz) each
trimmed and seasoned
3 tablespoons olive oil
500 g (1 lb) baby carrots, scraped and diced
300 g (11 oz) baby turnips, scraped and diced
12 baby onions, peeled and diced
1 celery heart, scraped and diced
500 g (1 lb) tomatoes, chopped
200 g (7 oz) salt pork, diced
4 cloves garlic, peeled and lightly crushed
1 bouquet garni
400 ml (14 fl oz) dry white wine

1 Brown the lamb steaks over a high heat in one tablespoon of the olive oil. Set aside.

2 In a large frying pan, fry the diced carrots, turnips, onions and celery in the remaining oil. Add the chopped tomatoes and salt pork.

3 Oil a casserole. Spread half the mixture on the bottom. Cover with the lamb steaks, and place the crushed garlic cloves and bouquet garni on top. Cover with the rest of the mixture.

4 Sprinkle with the white wine. Cover and leave to cook in a preheated oven at 190°C (375°F), Gas Mark 5, for an hour. Remove from the oven, take off lid and reduce on the top of the stove over a medium head for 10 minutes.

CANARD DU PAYS NIÇOIS
DUCK NIÇOISE

SERVES 4
1 × 2-2.5 kg (4½-5½ lb) Barberry duck
salt and pepper
2 tablespoons olive oil
1 kg (2 lb) tomatoes, skinned and chopped
2 red peppers, cored, seeded and finely diced
½ stick celery, chopped
2 carrots, finely diced
4 cloves garlic, crushed
400 ml (14 fl oz) dry white wine
200 g (7 oz) small black olives

1 Season the inside of the duck with salt and pepper. Place the duck in a lightly oiled roasting tin and cook in a preheated moderately hot oven, at 200°C (400°F), Gas Mark 6, for 30 minutes.

2 Meanwhile, heat the remaining oil in a saucepan large enough to hold the duck. Fry the tomatoes, peppers, celery and carrots in the oil, then stir in the garlic.

3 Make a space in the middle of this mixture and add the duck. Pour on the white wine and cook covered, for 1 hour. Add the olives and cook for 15 minutes more.

4 Remove the duck and keep it hot on a serving dish. Skim off any fat from the stock, then increase the heat and reduce the liquid to a sauce. Serve with the duck. Rice or fresh pasta makes a good accompaniment.

CANARD DU PAYS NIÇOIS

RÔTI DE PORC À LA SAUGE

RÔTI DE PORC À LA SAUGE
ROAST PORK WITH SAGE

Have your butcher bone the pork, but not roll and tie it.

SERVES 6

1.5 kg (3 lb) boned top shoulder of pork, fat
and skin removed
5 cloves garlic, crushed
14 leaves of fresh sage
salt and pepper
2 tablespoons lard
1 large carrot, sliced
1 small onion or shallot, peeled and chopped
5 tomatoes, skinned and chopped
500 ml (18 fl oz) dry white wine
vegetable or chicken stock (see method)

1 Place the pork shoulder on the work surface and top with 3 cloves of garlic and 4 sage leaves. Sprinkle with salt and pepper. Roll the joint, enclosing the garlic and sage, and tie it in a neat shape. Melt 1 tablespoon of the lard in a saucepan large enough to hold the pork. When it is hot, add the pork and brown slowly on all sides. Remove and set aside.

2 Melt the remaining lard in the pan. Add the carrot, onion and remaining sage and garlic and cook for 4 to 5 minutes. Stir in the tomatoes. Return the pork to the pan, placing it on top of the vegetables. Cook for 5 minutes.

3 Pour the white wine over the pork and add sufficient stock to cover the meat. Bring to the boil, lower the heat and simmer, covered, for 1¼ hours. The pork should remain covered by liquid at all times to prevent it drying out.

4 When the pork is cooked, remove it from the pan and keep it hot on a serving dish. Skim off any fat from the surface of the stock, then increase the heat and reduce the liquid by about two thirds. Serve with the pork. Courgettes go well with this dish.

SAUCISSES À LA PROVENÇALE
SAUSAGES, PROVENÇAL STYLE

SERVES 4

2 tablespoons olive oil
2 onions, peeled and chopped
2 cloves garlic, peeled and chopped
1 aubergine, sliced
2 courgettes, sliced
4 large tomatoes, peeled, seeded and chopped
salt and pepper
1 bay leaf
1 sprig of rosemary
1 sprig of thyme
4 large pork sausages

1 Salt the sliced aubergine and courgettes for 30 minutes, rinse and drain well.

2 Heat the olive oil in a saucepan and add the chopped onions, garlic, aubergine and courgettes. Cover the pan and simmer for about 5 minutes. Then add the tomatoes, salt, pepper and herbs, and 'sweat' for a few minutes longer.

3 Remove the lid and continue cooking for a little longer until all the liquid has evaporated.

4 Meanwhile, prick the sausages with a fork and cook under a moderate grill for 10 minutes, turning them frequently.

5 Place the vegetables on a serving dish and arrange the sausages on top. Serve very hot.

CERVELLES D'AGNEAU AU PERSIL
LAMBS' BRAINS WITH PARSLEY

SERVES 3
500 g (1 lb) lambs' brains
2–3 rashers streaky bacon
6 tablespoons dry white wine
2 small onions, peeled and sliced
2 small carrots, peeled and sliced
1 tablespoon chopped parsley
juice of ½ lemon

1 Wash the brains in cold water and remove as much of the skin and membranes as possible. Soak for 2 hours in luke-warm water to remove the blood.

2 Wrap the rashers of bacon round the brains and simmer in the dry white wine with the vegetables and chopped parsley for 30 minutes. Drain and sprinkle with lemon juice.

3 Serve with fried parsley and steamed or boiled potatoes and sprinkle with extra chopped parsley if you wish.

SAUTÉ DE VEAU
VEAL SAUTÉ

SERVES 4
3 tablespoons olive oil
750 g (1½ lb) shoulder of veal, cubed
1 large onion, peeled and sliced
2 cloves garlic, peeled and finely chopped
1 tablespoon plain flour
200 ml (⅓ pint) dry white wine
1 red pepper, grilled, peeled and sliced
500 g (1 lb) tomatoes, peeled, seeded and quartered
salt and pepper

1 Heat the oil in a casserole, add the meat, onion and garlic, and fry gently for 3 minutes.

2 Sprinkle with flour, stir and add the white wine. Finally, add the red pepper and tomatoes, and season with salt and pepper. Cover and simmer for 45 minutes. Serve on a bed of boiled rice and garnish with parsley.

PAUPIETTES DE VEAU AUX OLIVES ET AUX OIGNONS
VEAL ROLLS WITH OLIVES AND ONIONS

SERVES 4
8 slices Parma ham
8 thin veal escalopes
3 tablespoons olive oil
225 g (8 oz) pickling onions, peeled
500 g (1 lb) tomatoes, peeled, seeded and quartered
1 teaspoon thyme
2 bay leaves
salt and pepper
150 ml (¼ pint) dry white wine
100 g (4 oz) green olives
100 g (4 oz) black olives
1 tablespoon chopped parsley to garnish

1 Wrap a slice of ham round each veal escalope, roll up into *paupiettes* and tie with fine string.

2 Warm the oil in a casserole and fry the onions until golden brown.

3 Add the *paupiettes*, tomatoes, thyme, bay leaves, salt and pepper. Pour the white wine on top, cover and simmer gently for 45 minutes.

4 Add all the olives and cook for a further 15 minutes.

5 Remove the string holding the *paupiettes* together just before serving, and sprinkle with chopped parsley. Serve with Spaghetti à la crème de basilic (see page 69).

PAUPIETTES DE VEAU AUX OLIVES ET AUX OIGNONS *(ABOVE)*
CERVELLES D'AGNEAU AU PERSIL *(BELOW)*

VEGETABLES

Vegetables are an integral part of Provençal cuisine and are unrivalled in spring and summer. There are also many regional dishes which can be eaten later in the year, and pasta also features as an accompaniment.

COURGETTES ET TOMATES FARCIES
STUFFED COURGETTES AND TOMATOES

This recipe can be varied using onions (shells only, first browned in a frying pan), aubergines and green or red peppers. Halve and hollow out the aubergines and halve the peppers and blanch for 5 minutes only.

SERVES 4
4 courgettes
salt
4 large tomatoes
8 rashers of bacon, rinded and finely chopped
2 onions, peeled and finely chopped
4 cloves garlic, peeled and finely chopped
2 tablespoons chopped parsley
2 tablespoons olive oil
2 eggs, beaten
40 g (1½ oz) fresh breadcrumbs
50 g (2 oz) Parmesan cheese, grated

1 Cut off both ends of the courgettes. Place in boiling salted water for 15 minutes and drain.

2 Meanwhile, cut off a slice from the top of the tomatoes, and carefully scoop out the flesh with a spoon. Salt the cases lightly and place upside down on a plate to drain. Reserve the 'lids' for later.

3 Lightly fry the bacon, onion, garlic and parsley with the scooped-out tomato flesh in the olive oil for 5 minutes.

4 Transfer this mixture to a bowl. Cut the courgettes in half lengthways and gently scoop out the flesh with a spoon. Add half the courgette flesh to the bacon and vegetables in the bowl, then add the eggs and breadcrumbs.

5 Fill the courgette halves and tomatoes with the prepared stuffing. Put the 'lids' back on the tomatoes and sprinkle the courgettes with Parmesan cheese. Place in an ovenproof dish and bake in a preheated oven, at 200°C (400°F), Gas Mark 6, for 20 minutes.

POMMES DE TERRE MISTRAL
POTATOES MISTRAL

SERVES 6
6 tablespoons olive oil
2 large onions, peeled and finely chopped
4 cloves garlic, peeled and finely chopped
4 large tomatoes, peeled, seeded and finely chopped
1 kg (2 lb) potatoes, peeled and sliced
salt and pepper
1 teaspoon chopped thyme
1 teaspoon chopped parsley
1 teaspoon chopped basil

1 Heat the oil in a large casserole and add the onions. Fry gently for 5 minutes taking care that the oil does not get too hot, then add the garlic and tomatoes. Cook for a further 10 minutes, then add the sliced potatoes.

2 Cover with water, season with salt, pepper and all the herbs. Cover with a lid and simmer on a low heat for 30 minutes.

COURGETTES ET TOMATES FARCIES

GÂTEAU D'ÉPINARDS
SPINACH CAKE

SERVES 4
200 g (7 oz) plain flour
2 eggs, beaten
200 g (7 oz) butter, softened
200 g (7 oz) soft cream cheese
5 tablespoons single cream
salt and pepper
1 pinch of nutmeg
350 g (12 oz) spinach

1 Sift the flour into a bowl and make a well in the centre. Put the eggs, butter, cream cheese and cream in the well and season with salt, pepper and nutmeg. Gradually incorporate the flour, mix well and add the spinach.

2 Pour into a greased ovenproof dish and bake in a moderate oven, at 180°C (350°F), Gas Mark 4, for 30 minutes.

BEIGNETS DE COURGETTES
COURGETTE FRITTERS

SERVES 8
6 small courgettes
salt
600 ml (1 pint) oil for deep frying
BATTER:
250 g (9 oz) plain flour
1 pinch of salt
1 tablespoon vegetable oil
15 g (½ oz) fresh yeast creamed with 2 tablespoons warm water
1 egg white, lightly beaten

1 First make the batter. Sift the flour and salt into a mixing bowl. Make a well in the centre, place the oil and creamed yeast in the well, and gradually incorporate the flour. Add the warm water and mix well. Add the egg white and stir. Leave for 2 hours before using.

2 Meanwhile, peel the courgettes and rinse in cold water. Slice lengthways and pat dry with paper kitchen towel. Salt lightly.

3 Dip each courgette slice in the batter and place in very hot oil until golden brown. Drain and place on paper kitchen towel to dry.

4 Arrange on a serving dish, and accompany with a dry white wine.

RATATOUILLE
PROVENÇAL RATATOUILLE

Cooked in the traditional way this dish is the very essence of Provence. It can be served hot or cold to accompany roast meat, or on its own – sometimes with grilled cheese or fried eggs on top.

SERVES 6
5 courgettes, peeled and sliced
2 aubergines, sliced
salt and pepper
3 onions, peeled and finely chopped
200 ml (⅓ pint) olive oil
2 large green peppers, grilled, peeled and sliced
1 kg (2 lb) tomatoes, peeled and quartered
6 cloves garlic, peeled and finely chopped
2 tablespoons chopped parsley
1 tablespoon chopped basil

1 Lightly salt the sliced courgettes and aubergines and allow to drain in a colander, or dry on kitchen paper.

2 Fry the onion lightly in some of the olive oil for 15 minutes. Transfer to a casserole. Fry the green pepper, tomato, courgette and aubergine in turn, for 15 minutes each time, draining and adding them to the casserole as you go. Replenish the pan with the olive oil as necessary.

3 Mix all the vegetables in the casserole, add the garlic, season with freshly ground pepper, and simmer for 30 minutes. Add the chopped herbs 5 minutes before serving.

RATATOUILLE

ARTICHAUTS À LA BARIGOULE

ARTICHAUTS À LA BARIGOULE
ARTICHOKES À LA BARIGOULE

SERVES 6
6 purplish artichokes, not too large
juice of 1 lemon
6 tablespoons olive oil
225 g (8 oz) mushrooms, chopped
1 tablespoon chopped fresh parsley
150 g (5 oz) pickled pork or smoked bacon,
chopped
2 cloves garlic, crushed
salt and pepper
150 g (5 oz) carrots, finely sliced
1 medium onion, finely sliced
1 bouquet garni
300 ml (½ pint) dry white wine
300 ml (½ pint) chicken stock or water
beurre manié: 25 g (1 oz) plain flour mixed with
25 g (1 oz) soft butter

1 Remove the stalks and the leaves at the base of each artichoke. Cut off the ends of the leaves. Remove the fibres and the hard parts of the heart using a small spoon. Sprinkle lemon juice on to the hearts to prevent discoloration.

2 Heat 3 tablespoons of the oil in a frying pan. Fry the mushrooms, parsley, pickled pork and garlic, seasoning the mixture with salt and pepper. Fill the artichokes with the mixture.

3 In a heavy casserole large enough to hold all the artichokes upright, add the remaining oil and fry the carrots and onion until golden. Add the bouquet garni and arrange the artichokes, upright and closely packed, on top. Add the wine and stock. Cook over a fairly high heat for 10 minutes. Cover, reduce the heat and simmer for 45 minutes.

4 Remove the artichokes and keep them hot on a serving dish. Discard the bouquet garni. Thicken the cooking liquid with the beurre manié, adding a little at a time and stirring constantly until the sauce is thick and smooth. Pour over the artichokes and serve immediately.

HARICOTS VERTS PROVENÇALE
FRENCH BEANS PROVENÇAL

SERVES 6
1 kg (2 lb) fine French beans
salt and pepper
200 ml (⅓ pint) Coulis de tomates (page 22)
2 cloves garlic, peeled and finely
chopped
1 tablespoon chopped parsley

1 Cook the beans in boiling salted water for 10 minutes. Drain and put in a saucepan with the tomato sauce and finely chopped garlic. Simmer for 20 minutes. Garnish with parsley just before serving.

POMMES DE TERRE ET HARICOTS VERTS EN SALADE
POTATO AND FRENCH BEAN SALAD

SERVES 4
1 kg (2 lb) potatoes, peeled and sliced
750 g (1½ lb) French beans
2 cloves garlic, peeled and finely sliced
VINAIGRETTE:
3 tablespoons olive oil
1 tablespoon wine vinegar
1 teaspoon Dijon mustard
salt and pepper

1 Place the potatoes in a pan and cook in boiling salted water for 15 minutes, adding the beans 5 minutes later. Allow to cool.

2 Meanwhile, make the vinaigrette by combining all the ingredients.

3 Arrange the vegetables in a salad bowl with the sliced garlic. Pour the vinaigrette over the vegetables and serve.

CHAMPIGNONS EN BOCAUX
BOTTLED MUSHROOMS

This preserve keeps for about 12 weeks and goes particularly well with cold roast meats.

SERVES 8
3 tablespoons wine vinegar
500 g (1 lb) mushrooms, peeled and sliced
1 clove garlic, peeled and sliced
200 ml (⅓ pint) olive oil
1 sprig of thyme
salt and pepper

1 Pour the vinegar into a saucepan and heat gently. Add the mushrooms and garlic, cook for 5 minutes and allow to cool.

2 Pour the cooled contents of the pan into a bottling jar containing the oil, and add the thyme, salt and pepper. When the contents are completely cold, put a lid on the jar and leave in a dark cool place.

HARICOTS BLANCS EN SAUCE TOMATE
BAKED BEANS

SERVES 4
500 g (1 lb) dried haricot beans
1 onion, peeled and quartered
1 clove garlic, peeled
450 ml (¾ pint) Coulis de tomates (see page 22)
2 tablespoons chopped basil
salt and pepper

1 Place the beans in a large pan, cover with cold water and boil, covered, for 5 minutes.

2 Drain the beans and return to the pan. Add the onion and garlic, and cover with boiling water. Cover and cook for a further 40 minutes.

3 Put the cooked beans in a casserole containing the tomato sauce. Add the chopped basil, season with salt and pepper and simmer for 15 minutes.

PAN BAGNAT
TOMATO SALAD SANDWICH

SERVES 4
4 large baps cut in half lengthways
Salade niçoise (see page 13)

The name literally means 'soaked bread', because the vinaigrette and vegetable juices must impregnate the bread. There are slight variations of pan bagnat throughout Provence. Outside the area around Nice, it is often made in a piece of *baguette*, but in and around Nice large, round, soft rolls are specially baked for this purpose.

Pan bagnat is more than just a snack and can constitute an entire meal such as lunch in itself.

PÂTES À LA TOMATE ET AUX CHAMPIGNONS
PASTA WITH MUSHROOMS IN TOMATO SAUCE

SERVES 6
2 litres (3½ pints) water
salt
500 g (1 lb) tagliatelle
225 g (8 oz) mushrooms, sliced
100 g (4 oz) butter, melted
300 ml (½ pint) Coulis de tomates (see page 22)
1 knob of butter
grated Gruyère cheese to serve

1 Bring the salted water to the boil in a large pan. Put the tagliatelle in it and cook, uncovered, for 10 minutes.

2 Meanwhile, toss the mushrooms in a frying pan with the melted butter.

3 Heat the tomato sauce, add the mushrooms and then the drained pasta, and toss well.

4 Put the pasta in a serving dish and add a knob of butter. Serve with a small bowl of grated Gruyère.

Pâtes à la tomate et aux champignons *(ABOVE)*
HARICOTS BLANCS EN SAUCE TOMATE *(BELOW)*

COEURS DE FENOUIL BRAISÉS

COEURS DE FENOUIL BRAISÉS
BRAISED FENNEL HEARTS

SERVES 4
4 fennel hearts, quartered
salt and pepper
3 tablespoons olive oil
3 cloves garlic, peeled and sliced
3 large onions, peeled and sliced
6 large tomatoes, quartered
6 tablespoons rosé wine, warmed
1 pinch of chopped marjoram

1 Cook the fennel hearts in salted boiling water for 10 minutes.

2 Pour the olive oil into an oval gratin dish with a lid and place over a medium heat. When it is hot, put the fennel hearts in with the garlic, onion and tomatoes. Add the warmed wine, marjoram and pepper. Cover and simmer for 1½ hours. Serve in the dish.

GNOCCHIS
SEMOLINA DUMPLINGS

SERVES 4
1.5 litres (2½ pints) milk
350 g (12 oz) semolina
1 pinch of ground nutmeg
2 tablespoons grated Cheddar cheese
2 eggs
25 g (1 oz) butter
TO GARNISH:
100 g (4 oz) melted butter
175 g (6 oz) grated Cheddar cheese

1 Bring the milk to the boil and gradually pour the semolina into it, stirring continuously with a wooden spoon for about 20 minutes. Add the nutmeg and grated cheese.

2 Remove from the heat and add the eggs, one by one.

3 Grease a tin with half the butter and spread the semolina mixture to a thickness of about 1 cm (½ inch).

4 Cut out the gnocchis using a small pastry cutter, 2.5 cm (1 inch) in diameter. Grease an ovenproof dish with the remaining butter and place the gnocchis in it.

5 Pour the melted butter over the top and sprinkle with grated cheese. Place in a moderate oven, at 190°C (375°F), Gas Mark 5, for 10 minutes or until golden brown.

SPAGHETTI À LA CRÈME DE BASILIC
SPAGHETTI WITH BASIL CREAM

SERVES 4
2 tablespoons double cream
1 tablespoon olive oil
1 clove garlic, peeled and crushed
2 tablespoons chopped basil
salt and freshly ground pepper
400 g (14 oz) spaghetti
50 g (2 oz) grated Parmesan cheese

1 First prepare the sauce by mixing together the cream, olive oil, crushed garlic, basil, salt and pepper in a bowl.

2 Cook the spaghetti in 1.5 litres (2½ pints) of boiling salted water. Drain.

3 Add the sauce to the drained spaghetti and sprinkle liberally with the grated Parmesan.

DESSERTS

Provence has plenty of sweet desserts and confectionery to round off the meal. Dried fruits and nuts stuffed with marzipan are traditional festive fare. Home-baked tarts filled with warmed honey and chopped walnuts also make delicious use of regional products. *Pâte de coings* is a delicious quince preserve; made in the autumn it will keep for many months and may be served as a dessert or as a relish. And for a refreshing summer dessert, peaches poached in wine and served with homemade water ice would make any occasion special.

GÂTEAU AU YAOURT À LA NOIX DE COCO
YOGHURT CAKE WITH COCONUT

The easiest way of measuring out the ingredients for this recipe is to use the empty 150 g (5.29 oz) yoghurt pot. Try using coconut yoghurt or mix the flavours with something different, like orange yoghurt, to vary this recipe. But remember if using a flavoured yoghurt to add slightly less sugar to the mixture. A sweet wine, such as Muscat de Beaumes de Venise, goes particularly well with this cake.

SERVES 8
1 pot natural yoghurt
2 yoghurt pots caster sugar
3 yoghurt pots self-raising flour, sifted
3 eggs
½ yoghurt pot desiccated coconut
¼ yoghurt pot vegetable oil

1 Pour the yoghurt into a mixing bowl and add the sugar. Stir well.

2 Add the flour and eggs, and mix well. Finally, pour in the desiccated coconut and oil.

3 Pour into a greased 20 cm (8 inch) round tin and bake in a preheated moderate oven, at 180°C (350°F), Gas Mark 4, for 45 to 50 minutes.

TARTES AU MIEL ET AUX NOIX
HONEY AND WALNUT TARTS

SERVES 6
275 g (10 oz) plain flour
1 teaspoon caster sugar
1 pinch of salt
150 g (5 oz) butter, softened and cut into pieces
about 6 tablespoons cold water
250 g (9 oz) walnuts
500 g (1 lb) clear honey, warmed

1 Sift the flour and add the sugar, salt, butter and sufficient water to form a firm dough. Mix in quickly with the fingertips, knead lightly and roll into a ball. Wrap and chill in the refrigerator for 2 hours.

2 Roll out the pastry on a lightly floured board and line six 10 cm (4 inch) flat tins with it. Prick the bases with a fork, and bake blind for 20 minutes in a preheated moderate oven, at 180°C (350°F), Gas Mark 4.

3 Meanwhile, chop the walnuts and mix with the warmed honey. Spread the mixture over the pastry case and return to the oven for a further 10 minutes.

4 Serve cold or lukewarm with a fine sweet wine such as a Monbazillac. When served warm these tarts are also delicious with Crème fraîche.

TARTES AU MIEL ET AUX NOIX

COMPOTE DE POMMES ET POIRES

COMPOTE DE POMMES ET POIRES
APPLE AND PEAR PURÉE

The subtle flavour of pear and vanilla adds interest to this simple apple purée.

SERVES 4
6 green eating apples, peeled and cored
6 pears, peeled and cored
6 tbls water
75-100 g (3-4 oz) caster sugar
1 vanilla pod

1 Cut the apples and pears into quarters and place in a pan containing the water, sugar and vanilla pod. Simmer gently for 15 minutes or until soft. Discard the vanilla pod.

2 When the fruit is soft, place in a liquidizer and work to a soft purée. Serve hot or cold with *langues de chat* biscuits.

MOUSSE AU CAFÉ
COFFEE MOUSSE

SERVES 4
6 *petits suisses*
4 tablespoons icing sugar
1 tablespoon coffee essence or granules
4 egg whites
chocolate coffee beans to decorate

1 Beat the *petits suisses* and add the icing sugar and coffee. Stir well.

2 Beat the egg whites until stiff and fold them into the mixture.

3 Decorate with chocolate coffee beans and serve with *boudoirs* biscuits.

CHICHI-FREGI
SWEET PASTRY RINGS

Traditionally, these rings are piped in circles, but it doesn't really matter if the circles do not hold during cooking.

SERVES 4 TO 6
500 g (1 lb) plain flour
pinch of salt
15 g (½ oz) fresh yeast
175 ml (6 fl oz) lukewarm water
2-3 tablespoons orange-flower water
oil for deep frying
caster sugar to serve

1 Sift the flour and salt into a large mixing bowl. Mash the yeast with the water in a second bowl and set aside until frothy.

2 Make a well in the centre of the flour and add the yeast mixture and orange-flower water. Gradually incorporate the flour until the mixture forms a fairly thin dough. Work until smooth, cover the bowl with a cloth and set aside in a warm place for about 2 hours or until doubled in bulk.

3 Heat the oil in a large frying pan. Fill a fairly large piping bag with dough and pipe the dough in circles about 10 cm (4 inches) across into the hot oil. When the circles are golden in colour, turn them over and brown the other side a little. Remove from the oil and drain on paper towels. If you want to make sure that the circles hold you can first pipe them onto greaseproof paper and then transfer them to the oil with a spatula. Sprinkle with sugar and serve immediately.

GRANITÉ AUX PÊCHES
PEACHES WITH FROZEN WINE

SERVES 4
4 ripe but firm peaches
250 ml (8 fl oz) Côtes de Provence wine
250 ml (8 fl oz) water
225 g (8 oz) caster sugar
1 pinch of cinnamon
8 leaves of fresh mint
GRANITÉ:
250 ml (8 fl oz) Côtes de Provence wine
120 ml (4 fl oz) fresh orange juice
100 g (4 oz) caster sugar

1 Boil some water in a pan and blanch the peaches for 30 seconds. Drain them, place under cold running water and peel.

2 Boil the wine with the water, sugar and cinnamon. Poach the peaches in this for 5 minutes. Remove the pan from the heat and allow the peaches to cool in the poaching liquid. When they are cool, transfer them to a plate and reserve the liquid.

3 Meanwhile, make the granité. Add the Côtes de Provence, orange juice and caster sugar to the cooled, reserved poaching liquid. Boil fast to reduce the liquid by one third, then allow to cool.

4 Pour the cold liquid into shallow trays and place in the freezer for 2 hours, until well frozen.

5 Remove the granité from the ice trays with a spoon, scraping it to make it look like shattered glass.

6 Arrange on a serving dish, put the peaches on top and decorate each peach with 2 leaves of fresh mint.

PÂTE DE COINGS
QUINCE CHEESE

Quince cheese will keep for several months or even a year provided it is well wrapped and left in a cool place so it is always worth making in quantity.

MAKES 3.5 KG (8 LB)
2 kg (4½ lb) ripe quinces, unpeeled
250 ml (8 fl oz) water
caster sugar (see method)

1 Wash and dry the quinces. Cut them into quarters and place in a large saucepan or preserving pan. Add the water. Bring to the boil, lower the heat, cover and simmer for about an hour, or until the quinces are soft.

2 Strain the quinces, discarding the cores and purée them in a blender or food processor, or by pressing through a fine sieve. Weigh the pulp, then place it in a clean saucepan. Add a weight of sugar equivalent to that of the fruit and simmer for 30 minutes, stirring constantly.

3 Remove a spoonful of the quince cheese and shake it. If the cheese slides off the spoon in a solid piece, it is cooked. Pour it into shallow tins and leave to cool. When cold, remove the cheese from the tins and cut into squares or fancy shapes. These may be eaten as they are or rolled in sugar.

CHICHI-FREGI *(ABOVE, RECIPE ON PAGE 73)*
PÂTE DE COINGS *(BELOW)*

NAVETTES *(ABOVE)*
DATTES, NOIX ET PRUNEAUX FARCIS *(BELOW)*

NAVETTES
BOAT-SHAPED CAKES FROM MARSEILLES

SERVES 8
65 g (2½ oz) softened butter
350 g (12 oz) caster sugar
pinch of salt
grated rind of 1 lemon
3 eggs
6 tablespoons water
750 g (1½ lb) plain flour
1 egg, beaten, to glaze

1 Place the butter, sugar, salt, lemon rind and eggs in a large bowl and beat thoroughly by hand or with an electric mixer until well combined. Beat in the water.

2 Sift the flour into a large mixing bowl. Make a well in the centre and add the butter mixture. Gradually incorporate the flour until a smooth dough is formed. Knead lightly.

3 Divide the dough into four pieces and roll each to a fairly thick sausage shape. Cut each 'sausage' into slices. Roll out each slice to a *navette* – an oval shape narrowed at each end.

4 Place the *navettes* on buttered baking sheets, keeping them well apart. Mark a cut along the length of each one with a knife leaving the ends uncut. Cover and leave for 2 to 3 hours.

5 Brush the *navettes* with beaten egg to glaze and bake in a preheated moderate oven, at 180°C (350°F), Gas Mark 4, for 15 to 20 minutes. The *navettes* should be a rich golden colour and slightly soft to the touch. Allow them to stand for a few minutes to firm, then transfer to wire trays to cool completely.

DATTES, NOIX ET PRUNEAUX FARCIS
DATES, WALNUTS AND PRUNES STUFFED WITH MARZIPAN

This dish is part of the 13 desserts served at Christmas in Provence. It goes well with a dry white wine. You can colour the marzipan yourself if you prefer, or even make your own, if you have the time, following any traditional recipe.

SERVES 18 TO 20
500 g (1 lb) dates
500 g (1 lb) prunes
500 g (1 lb) walnuts
225 g (8 oz) white marzipan
225 g (8 oz) pink marzipan
225 g (8 oz) green marzipan
fine caster sugar to decorate

1 Slit the dates and prunes and remove the stones. Shell the walnuts, taking care not to break any of the two halves.

2 Prepare thin strips of white marzipan and insert these in the dates, leaving a fine white ridge showing.

3 Prepare thin strips of pink marzipan and insert these in the prunes, leaving a fine pink ridge showing.

4 Prepare thin strips of green marzipan and sandwich these between two halves of walnut.

5 Sprinkle the little ridges of marzipan that have been left showing with very fine caster sugar.

6 Arrange on three dessert plates, making three pyramids with the different fruits and nuts; or for a more simple occasion serve a selection on the plate.

INDEX